W9-ANX-079

HISTORY IN PICTURES

FOCUS ON

THE HARLEM RENAISSANCE

DR. ARTIKA R. TYNER

Lerner Publications ◆ Minneapolis

LETTER FROM CICELY LEWIS

Dear Reader,

Imagine being in an argument with a classmate and the teacher asks what happened. Your classmate tells their version of the story, but you don't get to share your version. Do you think this is fair? Well, this is what has happened throughout history.

CICELY LEWIS

This series looks at different events in US history with a focus on photos that help tell stories of people from underrepresented groups.

I started the Read Woke challenge in response to the needs of my students. I wanted my students to read books that challenged social norms and shared perspectives from underrepresented and oppressed groups. I created Read Woke Books because I want you to be knowledgeable and compassionate citizens.

As you look through these books, think about the photos that have captured history. Why are they important? What do they teach you? I hope you learn from these books and get inspired to make our world a better place for all.

Yours in solidarity,

—Cicely Lewis, Executive Editor

TABLE OF CONTENTS

Think critically about the photos throughout this book. Who is taking the photos and why? What is their viewpoint? Who are the people in the photos? What do these photos tell us?

There are so many important people and events in the Harlem Renaissance that we are not able to include them all in this book. After finishing this book, learn more about how to get involved. There are tips on page 25 to help you get started.

Smalls Paradise was owned by Ed Smalls (*center*). It was a popular club during the Harlem Renaissance.

THE REBIRTH OF CHANGE

RENAISSANCE **MEANS "REBIRTH."** The Harlem Renaissance birthed a group of Black artists, leaders, and activists. Two generations from slavery, they were determined not to be bound by the chains of racism, segregation, and discrimination. They had a vision of freedom. They would use the arts and activism to gain political, social, and economic rights. The National Association for the Advancement of Colored People (NAACP) is a famous organization that was founded in Harlem. It fights for civil rights for Black people. The NAACP and those active in the Harlem Renaissance came together from about 1918 to 1937 to create a new chapter in history.

Harlem Renaissance artists used their creativity and intelligence to reimagine the future while celebrating their cultural roots. Langston Hughes described this in his poem, "I, Too." He shared a vision of equal rights for Black Americans, especially the working class. African roots influenced the sound of jazz music. Playing the trumpet, Louis Armstrong created a new harmony of justice and freedom. Nella Larsen wrote books in which her characters explore their racial identities. Many other artists showed the power of Black excellence. Their work has left a lasting legacy. Over a century later, it has inspired a new generation of Black artists to build a more just and inclusive society. Modern artists are building a new Black Renaissance.

Entertainers from Smalls Paradise in 1929

CHAPTER 1
HARLEM RESHAPES HISTORY

HARLEM IS IN UPPER MANHATTAN, NEW YORK CITY. It was designed for the upper-class white community during the 1880s. A small Black population was living there. As the Black community grew, new housing was built and opportunities opened for people to move into the neighborhood. By the 1900s, additional Black American families also made Harlem their home. The Black community built its own cultural center with churches, businesses, and stores.

A busy street in
Harlem in the 1900s

About six million Black Americans moved during the Great Migration.

CHAPTER 2
ART FOR THE PEOPLE, BY THE PEOPLE

DURING THE GREAT MIGRATION (1916–1970), MANY BLACK PEOPLE MOVED FROM THE SOUTH TO URBAN AREAS ACROSS THE UNITED STATES, AND OTHERS MIGRATED TO OTHER COUNTRIES. They moved in hopes of finding a better future, working in places from offices to factories. The North promised better jobs, housing, health care, and education. But the reality was that the Black community continued to face poverty and racism. No matter where Black people lived, white people in power enforced segregation and discrimination. They treated Black people as second-class citizens.

Black artists resisted racism and fought for fair treatment. The arts served as a tool for self-expression and community empowerment. Writer and educator Alain Locke taught artists to express their culture and celebrate their African roots. He was central to the movement.

Alain Locke edited a book on Black art and literature. It was published in 1925.

Bessie Smith performs onstage with a group of dancers.

CHAPTER 3
REIMAGINING A NEW WORLD

I N THE EARLY 1920S, HARLEM WAS A PLACE TO CHASE YOUR DREAMS. Writers, musicians, and celebrities came together to build this new community. They expressed the importance of being Black and proud. They also celebrated the courage of Black people despite the challenges they faced. Their art and activism were tools to improve their lives and achieve the promise of equality. Art also preserved their African cultural history and traditions. The NAACP lobbied

> "Perhaps the mission of an artist is to interpret beauty to people—the beauty within themselves."

—LANGSTON HUGHES

Congress to pass a law that would make lynching illegal. They also fought in the courts on cases to stop segregation and voting restrictions.

The Writers

Harlem Renaissance writers criticized unfair practices and fought for equitable treatment.

Langston Hughes was a poet, novelist, and playwright. He began writing poetry in high school. Hughes broke boundaries with his poetry. He also called for Black artists to embrace their racial identity.

Langston Hughes is known for his portrayal of Black life.

Zora Neale Hurston published four novels.

Claude McKay often wrote about racial and economic inequality.

Zora Neale Hurston studied African American and Caribbean folklore. She is best known for her novel *Their Eyes Were Watching God*. Her work focused on the culture of rural Black communities in the South.

Claude McKay wrote the poem "If We Must Die." It challenged racial violence, during the Red Summer of 1919, a time when white people rioted against Black people across the country. He was later named Jamaica's national poet.

REFLECT

Langston Hughes wrote for justice. Bessie Smith sang to raise awareness. How can you use your gifts to make a difference?

Louis Armstrong composed more than fifty songs.

Duke Ellington was a popular jazz artist.

Bessie Smith recorded 160 songs.

Anne Spencer published over thirty poems. Her poems focused on the humanity and complexity of Black women. These poems influenced the womanism movement, or the movement for equal rights for Black women.

The Musicians

Jazz and blues were created by Black Americans. Musicians combined the musical roots of Africa with new sounds and rhythms.

Louis Armstrong was one of the most famous musicians in the world. He made jazz music come alive when he played the trumpet.

Gladys Bentley was a blues singer and performer. She performed for large audiences.

Duke Ellington was a pianist and bandleader. He also composed thousands of songs.

Bessie Smith was called the Empress of the Blues. Through her songs, she told the story of everyday people and their struggles.

MOTHER OF THE BLUES

Ma Rainey influenced the music of the Harlem Renaissance. She was called the Mother of the Blues. She recorded nearly one hundred songs. Rainey mentored famous musicians like singer Bessie Smith. Rainey was inducted into the Rock and Roll Hall of Fame in 1990.

Ma Rainey performs with her band in 1924.

Paul Robeson acting in *Othello* in 1942

Aaron Douglas painting in the 1970s

Augusta Savage smiles with her sculpture of an antelope.

The Actors

Performers of the Harlem Renaissance brought life to characters and advocated for civil rights.

Paul Robeson was a singer, actor, and activist. He used his fame to speak out against racial injustices and violence.

Josephine Baker was a global superstar. She performed on Broadway. She brought the experience of Black culture, life, and art to the world.

The Artists

Harlem Renaissance artists used their art to draw attention to Black American life.

Aaron Douglas studied African art. His paintings celebrated Black cultures.

Augusta Savage was a sculptor and art teacher. She used her artistry to honor key African American leaders like W. E. B. Du Bois and Marcus Garvey.

BLACK HISTORY

Arturo Alfonso Schomburg (*below*) was a historian and activist. A teacher of his once told him that Black people have no history. He proved his teacher wrong by compiling Black history. He cofounded the Negro Society for Historical Research. His collection is at the Schomburg Center for Research in Black Culture, a research library that's part of the New York Public Library system.

Thousands of Black Americans marched in the Silent Protest Parade of 1917.

CHAPTER 4
ARTS AND SOCIAL CHANGE

IN HARLEM THE ARTS SHAPED A MOVEMENT FOR RACIAL JUSTICE. Artists and activists helped to raise awareness and mobilize change for generations to come. As Black Americans migrated north, white people created tensions in the workplace and community. The year 1917 was marked with violence against the Black community. In East Saint Louis, Illinois, a labor dispute led to a racial massacre. For three days, white people beat and killed Black people.

Hundreds of Black people were murdered. Another six thousand people became homeless after their homes were burned down.

The Silent Protest Parade of 1917 was a protest to challenge this tragedy. Nearly ten thousand Black Americans marched in Harlem. A band of drummers led the group. The NAACP leaders and organizers including W. E. B. Du Bois and James Weldon Johnson followed in the procession. Children and women dressed in white marched behind them. They wore

W. E. B. Du Bois was a historian, author, and activist.

> "A people without the knowledge of their past history, origin and culture is like a tree without roots."
>
> —Marcus Garvey

white to symbolize the innocence of those killed in East Saint Louis. They marched in silence holding signs that read, "Make America Safe for Democracy" and "Thou Shalt Not Kill." This was one of the first mass protests in US history.

Black Americans who migrated north continued to face racial terror. The summer of 1919 was called the Red Summer. White mobs led riots in about twenty-five cities. There were also ninety-seven lynchings recorded. The violence spread to Washington, DC. A Black veteran was killed, and four days of racist mob violence followed. The mobs killed an estimated forty Black people, and many were injured.

REFLECT

The Harlem Renaissance addressed challenges like racism and poverty. What are the challenges facing your community? How do you think this answer varies depending on your race, class, gender, where you live, and other factors?

Millions of people around the world spoke out for racial justice in 2020.

Over one hundred years later, racial violence is still a threat to the Black community. Black American men are two and a half times more likely to be killed by the police than white men.

In 2020 a worldwide movement for racial justice started after the murder of George Floyd at the hands of a white police officer. During his arrest, a white officer held his knee on Floyd's neck. Floyd repeatedly said that he could not breathe. He stopped breathing and died under the officer's knee. Millions of people around the world took to the streets to protest.

PROTESTING POLICE BRUTALITY

Malcolm X (*right*) took a stand against police brutality in Harlem. In 1957 Johnson Hinton was severely beaten by the police and taken into custody at the police station despite needing medical attention. Malcolm X led a protest in front of the police station demanding medical treatment for Hinton. When his demands were met, he dispersed the huge crowd with a wave of his hand.

Performer Nick Cannon and Black Lives Matter of Greater New York cofounder Chivona Newsome speak at a racial justice protest in 2020.

After the murder of Floyd, artists and celebrities united to take a stand and demand change worldwide. Rapper LL Cool J used his talents to express support for Black Lives Matter and lift his voice for justice. Artists Mr. Detail Seven and Bankslave painted a mural of Floyd.

A new Black Renaissance is emerging where Black creators unite to demand freedom, justice, and equality.

TAKE ACTION

Learn more about modern Black creators, such as Amanda Gorman, Janelle Monáe, Jason Reynolds, Daveed Diggs, Viola Davis, and many more.

Take an art class, and create a piece that shares the message of justice and freedom.

Read a biography about one of the profiled leaders like Josephine Baker or Claude McKay.

Take a virtual tour of Harlem.

TIMELINE

1916 The Great Migration starts as Black Americans migrate from the rural South to other urban cities and to countries outside of the US.

1918 Marcus Garvey begins publishing a newspaper that highlights the achievements of the Black community.

1918–1937 Black arts from music to poetry create a new cultural experience in Harlem called the Harlem Renaissance.

1919 White supremacists in more than three dozen cities kill Black people during racial violence and terrorism. This period was called the Red Summer. Claude McKay writes the poem "If We Must Die" to honor the courage and strength of the Black community.

1921 Langston Hughes's first poem is published.

1925 Alain Locke's anthology, *The New Negro*, is published. It documents the history of the Harlem Renaissance.

1937 Zora Neale Hurston publishes her second book, *Their Eyes Were Watching God*.

PHOTO REFLECTION

This 2015 photo shows people protesting by holding a sign showing a drawing of Malcolm X with his quote, "Freedom by any means necessary." What is your reaction to this photo? Is this quote still relevant? If so, in what ways is progress still needed? How might your background and experiences affect your opinion?

Take or draw a picture about what freedom means to you. How can you stand up for freedom and equity?

GLOSSARY

BLACK LIVES MATTER: a global movement to promote justice, freedom, and liberty for Black people

BLACK RENAISSANCE: the third cultural movement following the Harlem Renaissance. Black creators use their intellect and creativity to fight for equality for Black people.

CIVIL RIGHTS: the rights of people to social, political, and economic equality

EQUALITY: the quality or state of being equal, or receiving the same treatment as others

EQUITY: fairness or justice in the way people are treated

GREAT MIGRATION: when many Black families migrated to cities in the North and outside the US for job and economic opportunities

MOVEMENT: a change in laws, policies, and society

RED SUMMER: the period during 1919 when race massacres occurred in major cities across the United States

RENAISSANCE: a rebirth of culture, arts, and literature

SEGREGATION: the forced separation of a group of people from another group of people

WOMANISM MOVEMENT: the fight for equality for Black women

SOURCE NOTES

11   Zachary Lamb, "Life according to Langston Hughes," National Endowment for the Arts, February 14, 2018, https://www.arts.gov/stories/blog/2018/life-according-langston-hughes.

20   LaShawn Routé Chatmon, "Deeply Rooted in Black History," National Equity Project, February 24, 2021, https://www.nationalequityproject.org/blog/black-historys-deep-roots.

READ WOKE READING LIST

Britannica Kids: Harlem Renaissance
https://kids.britannica.com/kids/article/Harlem-Renaissance/353232

Grimes, Nikki. *Legacy: Women Poets of the Harlem Renaissance*. New York: Bloomsbury, 2021.

Grimes, Nikki. *One Last Word: Wisdom from the Harlem Renaissance*. New York, Bloomsbury, 2017.

Kiddle: Harlem Renaissance
https://kids.kiddle.co/Harlem_Renaissance

Nichols, Hedreich. *The Harlem Renaissance*. Ann Arbor, MI: Cherry Lake, 2022.

PBS: "The Harlem Renaissance"
https://www.thirteen.org/wnet/newyork/laic/episode5/topic2/e5_t2_s2-hr.html

Smith, Sherri L. *What Was the Harlem Renaissance?* New York: Penguin Workshop, 2021.

Tyner, Dr. Artika R. *Amanda Gorman: Inspiring Hope with Poetry*. Minneapolis: Lerner Publications, 2022.

Weatherford, Carole Boston. *Unspeakable: The Tulsa Race Massacre*. Minneapolis: Carolrhoda Books, 2021.

INDEX

PHOTO ACKNOWLEDGMENTS

Image credits: Bettmann/Getty Images, p. 5; Library of Congress, pp. 6, 11, 13, 16 (top), 19; Schomburg Center for Research in Black Culture, Photographs and Prints Division, The New York Public Library. "Harlem Tenement in Summer" The New York Public Library Digital Collections. 1935–1939, p. 7; Everett Collection/Shutterstock.com, p. 8; Carl Van Vechten Papers Relating to African American Arts and Letters Collection. Manuscripts and Archives, Yale University Library, p. 9; Anthony Barboza/ Archive Photos/Getty Images, p. 10; The Beinecke Rare Book and Manuscript Library, Yale University, p. 12 (right) (left), 13 (middle), 18; Carl Van Vechten, restored by Adam Cuerden/Wikimedia Commons (Public Domain), p. 13 (bottom); Michael Ochs Archives/Getty Images, p. 14 (15); Robert Abbott Sengstacke/Getty Images, p. 16 (middle); National Archives, p. 16 (bottom); Science History Images/Alamy Stock Photo, p. 17; Michal Urbanek/ Shutterstock.com, p. 21; CORBIS/Corbis/Getty Images, pp. 22-23; Noam Galai/Getty Images, p. 24; Gina Kelly/Alamy Stock Photo, p. 27.

Cover: JP Jazz Archive/Redferns/Getty Images.

Content Consultants: Professor Daylanne English and Dr. Terry Anne Scott

Lerner Publications Company
An imprint of Lerner Publishing Group, Inc.
241 First Avenue North
Minneapolis, MN 55401 USA

For reading levels and more information, look up this title at www.lernerbooks.com.

Main body text set in Aptifer Sans LT Pro.
Typeface provided by Linotype AG.

Designer: Viet Chu
Lerner team: Martha Kranes, Sue Marquis

Library of Congress Cataloging-in-Publication Data

Names: Tyner, Artika R., author.
Title: Focus on the Harlem Renaissance / Dr. Artika R. Tyner.
Description: Minneapolis : Lerner Publications, [2023] | Series: History in pictures (Read woke books) | Includes bibliographical references and index. | Audience: Ages 9–14 | Audience: Grades 4–6 | Summary: "The Harlem Renaissance combined art and social change. Readers will discover leaders and artists of the time, the Silent March, and why many say that we are living in a Black Renaissance"— Provided by publisher.
Identifiers: LCCN 2021047405 (print) | LCCN 2021047406 (ebook) | ISBN 9781728423487 (library binding) | ISBN 9781728462899 (paperback) | ISBN 9781728461427 (ebook)
Subjects: LCSH: African American arts—New York (State)—New York—20th century— Juvenile literature. | Harlem Renaissance—Juvenile literature.
Classification: LCC NX512.3.A35 T96 2023 (print) | LCC NX512.3.A35 (ebook) | DDC 700.89/9607307471—dc23/eng/20220124

LC record available at https://lccn.loc.gov/2021047405
LC ebook record available at https://lccn.loc.gov/2021047406

Manufactured in the United States of America
1-49186-49317-2/25/2022